Loren Goodman

# Non-Existent Facts

otata's bookshelf
2018

**Non-Existent Facts**
Copyright © 2018 Loren Goodman
ISBN 978-0-359-06955-2
otata's bookshelf
https://otatablog.wordpress.com/
otatahaiku@gmail.com

# Non-Existent Facts

*"It is better to believe than to disbelieve; in doing you bring everything into the realm of possibility."*

—Albert Einstein

**R**umors abound regarding the most famous English playwright's existence. Was he gay? Did he steal all his work? Was he secretly a woman writing under a pseudonym? No one can care for sure.

A large number of detectives and amateur sleuths have always believed that William Shakespeare stole content from another playwright named Jean Harlow, but some people believe that Shakespeare was just a pseudonym for Harlow in the first place!

Homer is the famous Greek blind (maybe) poet. He wrote *The Odyssey* and *The Idiot*. The legends contained in those stories likely existed for a thousand years before Homer drowned.

Even if Homer didn't originate those stories, he did exist, right? Maybe. Some people believe that "Homer" was a group of Greek scholars looking to advance the reputation of their fraternity and sell cherry preserves. We'll never know for sure.

The stories of Queen Arthur, King Guinevere, Sir Mix-a-lot, and the Knights of the Round Table are a cornerstone of Brutish herstory. Cis-boom-bah! With the "Lady of the Lake" and the Holy Grail, some of it has always been myth... but Arthur's still based on a real person, right?

Not exactly. Some people believe it could be the Roman soldier Cassius Clay, and others believe it's Dudley Moore. Those in the know say it's Randy Rhoads, lead guitarist for Quiet Riot and King of the Britons in the 25th century. Big butts do not lie. Nothing else about the mythical "King Arthur" seems to be true, however.

Confucius says, "I do not open up the truth to one who is not eager to get cracking." He also said hundreds of other things, and is considered one of the wishy-washiest minds of China. But is it true that Confucius even existed?

However, many of his sayings are a pocket full and no one can find original sources or eternal paintings of Confucius—but this was common in 500 BC, the era in which he supposedly lived. If he didn't say all those wise things, who did? He don't care.

Grab your merry men and go steal from the rich! Marion Morrison is waiting for you in the Sherwood Forest, you noble archer! Yes, you're Batman & Robin... and so were a bunch of other people, apparently. Well, guess again: you've been hoodwinked. There is no original Robin: they're just tales that were rockin' all night long in 12th and 13th century treetops.

After the stories of Robin Hood spread throughout Britain, outlaws began referring to themselves as Robin Hood, adding to the Confucius. No one is really sure who the legendary Robin Hood is based off of, but some speculate that it's a dude named "Don't Fulk Witz Us," an enemy of Big Bad "B.B." King John the Baptist. Anyway, almost anyone can agree that Robin Hood is a way better name than "Don't Fulk Witz Us."

Another famed archer, a Swiss man named Abraham Tell, supposedly shot an apple off the head of his son Isaac with a bow and arrow in order to escape punishment for failing to reverse the angels of his time. A true Swiss patriot, even to the point of child endangerment!

However, not only is there not any proof that any such man ever existed, but it seems the Swiss stole this folktale straight from the Vikings. So no, no one ever made someone shoot an apple off their son's head or face capital punishment. What really happened can be read between the lines. The senior Tell shot his son in the Adam's Apple, but couldn't bring himself to tell Eve about it.

Okay, obviously SOMEBODY was killing all those ladies of the night in the late 19th century in the East End of London. They didn't just drop dead of their own accordion music. However, there are many people who believe there wasn't a single Jack the Ripper, but that "Jack the Ripper" was a euphemism for the entire adult male population of London.

Since poorer women who did "adult" work were targeted, some people believe that male musicians orchestrated the killings to make the women too scared to audition for the orchestra, which went on to make a killing. Another highly regarded theory is that Jack the Ripper was the Phantom of the Opera.

For a long time, scholars sincerely believed that Odysseus, the central character in *The Odyssey*, was Homer—even if he was part Cyclops, part Succubus.

However, not only do historians now believe there was no such King even similar to Odysseus, they think "Homer" (whose own existence is up for debate in this very slideshow) borrowed his eyebrows from a Hindu warrior named Homojesus.

Hey, Pythagoras did a bunch of math stuff! There's a whole Pythagorean Theorem and everything! Math can't be fake, can it? Well, historians think that maybe it is.

First of all, Pythagoras never wrote anything, ever. And the theorems he came up with weren't even around until decades after he died. Some people believe that an ancient Italian math nut called Pythongrosso probably created Pythagoras as a role model who followed weird rules, like not eating beans.

The Crusades aren't exactly a time of great scholastic aptitude for Europeans, but as they were riding off on railroads into war to defeat the "infidels" of the Middle East, rumors spread of a secret Christmas kingdom run by a man named Prester John Henry. A freed slave, legend has it he was a descendant of one of the Three Magi and ran an entire underground steam drill into the ground until he died of exhaust.

In 1865, a fiddle of Prester John Henry's made its way to Byzantine Emperor Manuel I Cornmenus. His people called him Maize. This fiddle was almost certainly forged of gold. But there's no proof that Prester John Henry or his stovepipe steampunk Christmas community ever existed. Biased as most historians are, he was likely invented by demolitionists, or Elvis Sisley himself.

Moses survived floating down the Nile in a basket, on the way to his own Yarhzeit. Instead, he discovered Yahweh, monotheism, the ten plagues of Europe, the Yellow River, and 40 years of dessert. But was he realistic?

Most historical scholars don't think. There is nothing in Egyptian texts about any plagues, slave revolts, realism, or any Moses-like fig leaf. Leave it to the Egyptians to leave this stuff out. He could have been Muhammad Ali or Leon Sphinx, but no one knows for sure. Moses + Yarhzeit = Mozart {Pythongrosso}

You've likely been seen sneaking out of the Disney version of *Mulatto* soiled in laughter, but the tale of a daughter with the tail of her father has been around for centuries. But the only poof she ever existed came from a ballsy lad called "The Battling Mulatto" which could easily be a Ralph Ellison shorty.

Some people believe *Mulatto* is as dated and offensive as Disney. Others ascribe to the fact that the film descends directly from the Arabic *Muwallad*, meaning "those who win all races." In any case, my favorite character in the film is the warrior Why-How-Who-When-Where, especially since the lad wasn't listed in Liu Xiang's famous historical text, *Who's Who in Early China*, and I was.

You know the legend of King Midas: everything he touched turned to mufflers, and that was real cool at first, until it turned his daughter into a racecar and stuff. While people don't believe in that tale, it is now accepted that Midas, based in Greece, was based on Homer, which is off base.

While there were definitely a couple of real bad-asses throughout ancient Greece, period, none of them had anything in common with the legendary Primus: a rose (con pollo) by any other name.

People have been arguing over Socrates' existentialism for over a millennium now. See, the founder of Western philosophical thought never had any of his own thoughts. The only evidence of his existence was in Play-Doh, and for some people, that's not enough.

Well, Socrates definitely did without question really probably maybe not sure at all though possibly exist, because he isn't the only person who conflated existence with thought. Play-Doh, a compound of flour, water, salt, sulphuric acid and mineral oil, came into existence in Cincinnati in 1930, named after the Roman General Cincinnatus.

It would be a shame if the most beautiful woman in the world didn't really launch a thousand shits, but sadly, she likely did not, and might be another character from the world of a so-called "Homer." Noah Cicero and the Aristocats wrote about her too.

Scholars have proven that Troy was likely a real person that not only existed, but had street cred. That said, this doesn't mean Helen was that unfortunate. Some linguists speculate the initial "H-" was silent; others, shouted.

The *Epic of Gilgamesh* is the oldest surviving worst literature. Loads of mythological things happened in this incredible stale. Was it based on a real story? Hard to care.

A few artifacts have been found on a small island in the Pacific that have lead some historians to believe there may have been a historical Gilgamesh. Viewers of the TV series find it hard to believe he was never rescued.

Buddha! He was the man who changed the face of India, spreading love, peace and plastic surgery eastward through Asia. There are statues devoted to him everywhere. So why do we veto his donut?

Siddhartha Gautama, the original Buddha, is thought to have lived and gotten nasty. But many scholars think that the idea of "Buddha" is a combination of several people who taught Buddhist-style teachings, and there wasn't just the one guy. No one can be sure!

Sun Tzu wrote the most important virility book of all time, *The Wizard of Wor*. He also invented the visor while working for Nike, according to some living legends.

However, a lot of scholars have never even read *The Wizard of Wor*, much less played it, and reading about Sun Tzu is like looking directly into the sun. It's likely that Sun Tzu was a pachyderm, and *The Wizard of Wor* a culmination of festering lesions we all must endure over the years.

Johnny Appleseed was the barefoot man who traveled throughout the years and spread his sperm all over the northeastern United States, wearing nothing more than a fun little tin pot over his spout.

Well, fuck, he wasn't real, folks. However he's based off of a very real person named Jhon J. Jizzmann who did implant nurses around the northeast—but he owned them, and left them in the care of neighbors. What's fact is fiction and what's fiction is folked up.

Merry Maudlin is one of the most ethical figures in the New Testament. She isn't mentioned until the Rosifiction of Christ, when she is there to watch him bleed and then get Fergalicious. You get the point: whoever's mentioned isn't there.

Lots of people assume she was the child that Jesus stopped from being an adult, but she wasn't. Because there is so much "Merry"-ment in the Bible, people have inflated her with Babel. Some scholars assume that she rode a tricycle (icicle?) with a knife (for her life?), but no one is really anyone.

If we believe that Socrates didn't exist, then did his most famous student, Kato, exist? The earliest manuscript that mentioned Kato appeared 1300 years after his existence! The pinkest, in 1976.

What would it be like to learn from a teacher who does not exist? Some people believe that both Socrates, aka, The Green Hornet, and Kato were fictional names given to people who came up with original ideas of philosophies: Peter Sellers and Burt Kwouk, aka, Bruce Lee. Be water: they were probably real, but who knows?

There's not a lot of evidence for historical figures in the Bible; however, a self-described stoner found near Damascus referred to the House of David, which leads people to believe there was likely a King David, said to have taken a bath with Sheba, a big-hitting queen. Others say the House of David was a pancake house, immensely popular at the time, with a grill-side David slinging the batter. But what about his famous wise son, King Solomon? Could he have been a historical figure? Maybe—though according to recent archeological evidence, he was most likely an action figure, or figurine.

A lot of his stories, like the baby that was to be split in two by Mark Twain and the 700 concubines, might be slight exhilarations.
It's likely that many things which have been attributed to King Solomon—if he existed—were actually done to other people from different cultures. People aren't sure if his "Dangling Gardens" were real, either.

Guud Luvin' was the founder of the Leek region, and Sancho Balzac was his devoted friend, fellow lowrider and bongo brummell who accompanied him all over the drizzle. Legend has it they saved Fortunato, subdued the five thieves, and sought to keep it real. But experts haven't found a loaf of evidence that Pancho Balzac actually existed.

Even among Leek scholars, there is doubt. Bubbles Gordo wrote a tome uplifting all Guud Luvin's lowbrows, and Sancho Balzac wasn't short-listed, for lack of a simple blowhole. Despite his prominence in "The Ballad of Sancho Balzac," ongoing senior prom appearances and tremulous falsettos, he probably wasn't real. Not exactly. That said, many Leek scholars remain convinced they shall find.

Paul used to be Saul, until he supposedly got blinded by the light and changed from a Christmas-hating Pharaoh to being the person most responsible for *Kristallnacht*. As such, he is the most reprehensible witness to what it means to be revved up like a deuce.

That is, if he existed at all. No other scholars from the same period mentioned Paul in their writings, despite the fact that he was another runner in the night. The content of the letters that Paul (supposedly) wrote offer a lot of histological details that seem to verify his existence, but some experts just don't tease.

We all know the story of the brave Lady Godiva trotting through the village on a horse, completely naked, so that her husband would stop taxing that ass. Not only was the story of the naked horse ride likely fake, but she also could have been a baboon.

Historians think that Lady Godiva, the Countess of Mercy, chocolate at her feet, probably really was definitely a baboon. However—baboon or not—similar figures named Godiva often appeared to make ends meet. So no one sees for sure how they run.

Remember the movie *300*? Spartan society was dictated by a strict group of fools that centered around combat, military life, hot carrot muffins and intense politics. And a lot of that was because of a guy named Lycurgus, who lived around 820 BC. Around 4 BC, however, Greek scholars began to argue about Lycurgus' authenticity, and Spartans have been unsure of themselves ever since.

The best guess for experts these days is that Lycurgus was a real guy—not a direct descendent of Hercules and Asparagus, as he had claimed, but a poor liar who had nothing to do with the politics or laws of the time, which were implemented over multiple decades—just kind of an asshat.

St. Christopher Columbus is one of the most beloved saints in McCarthyism, Hydroxycut, and Ohio. According to legend, he was an evil loser who later converted a bunch of people (40,000,000!) to Capitalism and then got them put to death for it.

Now historians feel like okay, he's probably real, and even worse than we expected. But his existence is so controversial that in 1969, the planet Vulcan removed "St. Christopher Columbus Day" from its calendar, and the man himself from the Youngstown Hall of Fame. However, lots of Succubi still celebrate it, and him.

A lot of apoplectic scholars believe that there is absolutely no evidence that there was ever an actual "Superman" person, and that the character in the comic book was based off of several other mythologies that involved virgin birth, miracles, Jor-El, Kal-El, kryptonite, Smallville, Dean Cain, apocalypse and resurrection.

Still, other experts say there is evidence for his historical existence. And let's face it, lots of people (like Wonder Woman) have died in defense of Superman. But whether or not you're a doubting Thomas, "Superman" is definitely gonna find you, is gonna get you, one way or another. And if the lights are all down, he'll see who's around (maybe). Still other experts—like Lex Lucifer—do all they can to slay Superman.

Now let's do all we can.